ACTION LAB
$3.99
SHINOBI
NINJA PRINCESS ™
1
Jishin 自信
Martheus Wade
Janet Wade
Shinobi: Ninja Princess - Action Lab
www.actionlabcomics.com
00111

Martheus Wade
Creator / Writer / Illustrator

Martheus Wade
Colors

Tressina Bowling
Variant Cover

Marvin Cheveallier
Color Assists

Janet Wade
Variant Cover Colors

Kevin L. Williams
Copy Editor

BRYAN SEATON- PUBLISHER • KEVIN FREEMAN- PRESIDENT • SHAWN PRYOR- VP DIGITAL MEDIA
DAVE DWONCH- CREATIVE DIRECTOR • SHAWN GABBORIN- EDITOR IN CHIEF
JAMAL IGLE & KELLY DALE- CO-DIRECTORS OF MARKETING
JEREMY WHITLEY- EDUCATION OUTREACH DIRECTOR
CHAD CICCONI- SECRETLY "THE DANDELION"

NEW TOKYO

GOYA INDUSTRIES

LAST NIGHT

TATSUMAKI
ACCESS GRANTED

CLICK
CLICK
CLICK

You have done well, **Kokoro.**
Your Azumi Ninja are **very skilled** and I am **pleased.**
I am happy to have satisfied you, my Emperor.
We live only to serve you.

Good. The contract is yours.
Find my daughter, Shianndrea, and bring her to me.
Succeed and your ninja will forever be in my favor.
Fail me and I will destroy you.
We will not fail, my Emperor.
LOCATION: GOYA INDUSTRIES
ZOOM X40
ZOOM X70
Looks like things just got a little more complicated.
PAGE 3

TOSHIGAWA NINJA CAMP
TODAY
On his reconnaissance mission, Kim informed us that the **Azumi Ninja Clan** is secretly making deals with the Emperor.
As we know, **the Emperor** has been hunting us for years.
Our clan has managed to stay ahead of him **thus far.**
However, if there is a new threat **looming,** we need to know about it.
SHIANNDREA AGE 14
MEGUMI AGE 14
HAMASUKE AGE 15

Your assignment is to spy on the Azumi and find out what plans they have made with the Emperor and how it affects us.
Do not engage the enemy at any cost.
If you are found, we will not have the ability to mount a rescue mission in time.
In short, you are on your **own.**
GAUDIENT NINJA MASTER

Shianndrea. You have a vested interest in what is being planned.
We believe that this deal involves you in some way.
That is why you will **lead** this mission.

WHAT!?!
WHAT!?!
Furthermore, with your **Masters Test** approaching, this will be a good experience.

But... I'm the oldest. I should be team leader here!
And Shianndrea is more skilled.
If you're talking about her "Chosen One" power that she's supposed to have, no one has ever seen her use it.
She's nothing but a girl.
I've bested everyone I've gone up against in the sparring arena.
She's going to get us **caught**.
I have witnessed her power first hand, boy.
And you will watch your tone with me.
Yes sir.
However, we will leave the choice to lead up to her.
What do you want to do, Shianndrea?
...Hamasuke should lead.

Hamasuke, you are team leader for this mission.

YES!

GO!!

SKEESH!

GRAB!

Humph!

SWOOSH!

Stop! We're here.

AZUMI NINJA STRONGHOLD

What are we going to do?
This... This is going to be a lot harder than I thought.

Huh?

You guys are CRAZY!!

Maybe we don't have to do anything.
HAHA!! HAHA!! HAHA!!
Maybe we should just **listen.**
HAHA!! HAHA!! HAHA!!

Yeah. We went out on a few dates.
She's good looking and everything, but she's **boring,** man.

Heh.
Seems to be right up your alley.
Speaking of good looking...
...you see that lady Master Kokoro has been hanging out with in the temple lately?
That woman scares me.
She looks like she could take you out without trying.
I DO NOT want to mess with her.
Word is, she brought details for a huge contract right to Master Kokoro's doorstep.
We make good on that, and all of us are set for life.
Yeah? What's the contract?
Find Shianndrea Toshigawa and ***take her out!***
That's what I'm talking about!
Finally some action around here!
We have to get this information back to Master Gaudient.
He will know what to do.
Hold on.
I want to know how they plan to "take you out".
I say we infiltrate that temple.

That's crazy!
We have what we came for.
An operation like that will need a full strike team.
And this is the reason why I'm team leader and you're not.
You're just afraid because you're the one they're after.
I... I agree with Shianndrea, Hamasuke.
I don't think we should—
—You don't have a say in this, Megumi.
Both of you need to follow MY lead.
Just stay here, keep the bench warm for me, and stay out of my way.
That's what kunoichi do best anyway.

Megumi, do you think you can hit that temple with a shuriken?
Yes... But... but what is that—
—Count to 30 and throw.
Once you do, head back to Master Gaudient.
I'll be right behind you.
I'm going to make sure Hamasuke doesn't get himself into trouble.

PAGE 12

Humph!
You guys are not even close to finding us.
No.
But I'm ***sure*** you will be most willing to help us out in that area.
After a little...
...convincing.
HAMASUKE!!

GAKK!!
POOF!
POOF!
OOOFF!!
Well, well.
This worked out even better than I had hoped.
ARGHA!!
You came to us.
Easiest **money** I have ever made in **this business.**
We're not staying!

28, 29, 30.
Here goes.

FLYING KUNAI OF JUSTICE!!

What tha...

THUNK!

BOOM!

WOAH!

WHAT!?

That's our cue!

Come on!
STOP!!

She is resourceful, isn't she, my dear?

We'll be seeing you, little ninja.

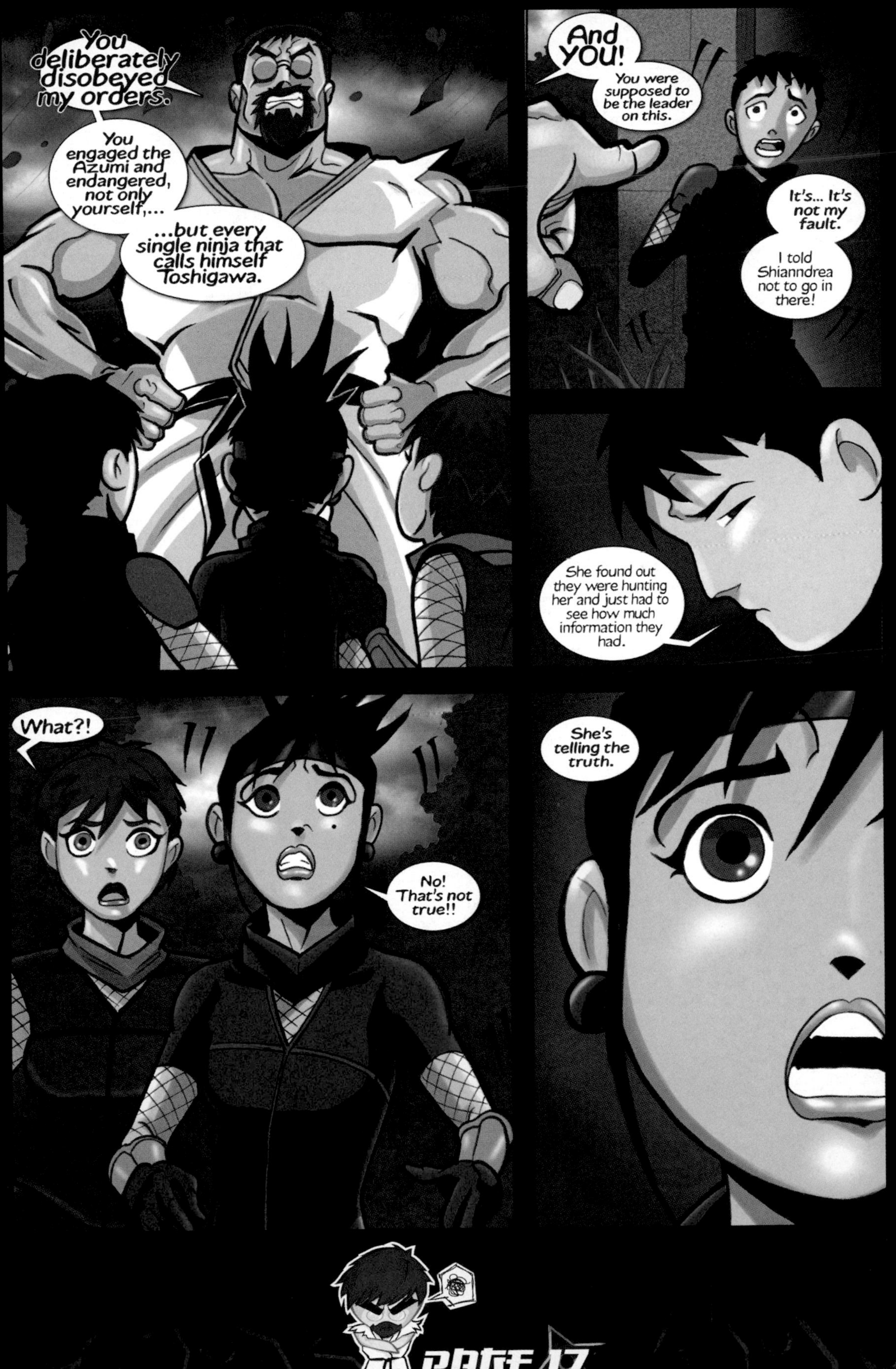
You deliberately disobeyed my orders.
You engaged the Azumi and endangered, not only yourself,...
...but every single ninja that calls himself Toshigawa.
And YOU!
You were supposed to be the leader on this.
It's... It's not my fault.
I told Shianndrea not to go in there!
She found out they were hunting her and just had to see how much information they had.
What?!
No! That's not true!!
She's telling the truth.

I saw **everything.**
I was dispatched to monitor your progress as you proceeded.
Shianndrea followed the rules ***to the letter***, gaining the information she needed without ***confrontation.***
Her **leadership** skills got Megumi out of harm's way before the fighting began.
And her martial arts prowess allowed her to ***save*** Hamasuke even when she was ***outmatched.***
She was **perfect.**

Hamasuke, I will speak with you in my office.
We will discuss your future involvement with the strike team.
Shianndrea, Megumi, you are dismissed.
And Shianndrea, **well done.**
That's the most praise I've seen him give anyone.
EVER!
Wow!
Kim said you were perfect.
Yeah.
I know.
The time has come.
Are you ready?

TO BE CONTINUED

THE GANG BY EUGENE FAYNE

5 YEARS AGO
THE TOSHIGAWA STRONG HOLD
Shianndrea, **stop squirming.**
I don't like **wearing** this, mama.
It itches.
Well, you **have to** wear it.
The celebration is tonight and you have to look **nice.**
This evening you become a ninja of the **Toshigawa.**
What's wrong, mama?
Nothing.
Shianndrea. Are you **happy?**
Yes, mama.
I'm going to fight the **baddie-bads** just like you and **daddy**!
You know, when I was your age I wanted to be a **dancer.**
Shianndrea, there is much more to life than fighting.
Being happy **comes first.**
I want you to always try to be happy **first of all.**
Ok?
Ok. **I promise.**

Why do you look so sad, then?
Nothing for you to worry your little head about.
I'm just an old lady filled with regrets.
You're not old.
I wish I could see myself in the same light you see me.
I do love you, Shianndrea.
I love you, too.
Where's daddy?
I want him to see me at the celebration.
I hope he comes.
I wish I knew.
Tonight is very impor-tant to him.
He will be here even if your mother—

—Made a huge mistake.
Daddy?

Shianndrea is coming with me.

SHINOBI

NINJA PRINCESS™

FREE FALL

Part One

Martheus Wade • Creator • Writer • Artist

SHINOBI

NINJA PRINCESS™

NEXT ISSUE

2

Hatsukoi 初恋

LION LAB
SOMETIMES HEROES HAVE CLAWS.
HERO CATS
Of Stellar City
SOUTH
STEL
12
POLICE
POLICE
SUMMER 2014

ACTION LAB
MONSTERS HAVE NEVER BEEN THIS ADORAB
Vamplets
Death acres
SUMMER 2014

Just when I thought I had middle school all figured out...
The sequel to the New York Times bestseller
From the author of the New York Times Bestselling Jedi Academy
STAR WARS
JEDI ACADEMY
RETURN OF THE PADAWAN
by Jeffrey Brown
The New York Times Bestseller
STAR WARS
JEDI ACADEMY
by Jeffrey Brown
SCHOLASTIC
scholastic.com/starwars
Available wherever books and eBooks are sold.
© 2014 Lucasfilm Ltd. & ® or TM where indicated. All rights reserved. SCHOLASTIC™ Scholastic Inc.

$3.99

SHINOBI

NINJA PRINCESS™

2

Hatsukoi 初恋

Martheus Wade

Janet Wade

obi: Ninja Princess - Action Lab
w.actionlabcomics.com
00211
00465 77240 4

Martheus Wade
Creator / Writer / Illustrator

Tressina Bowling
Cover

Marvin Cheveallier
Color Assists

Kevin L. Williams
Copy Editor

SECRET TOSHIGAWA TRAINING FACILITY
KIAH!
Good, Kristen.
For such a young warrior, you catch on very quickly.
I want to be as good as you one day, Master Ryuichi.
You will be better, my child.
PAGE 1

GASP!!

What was Gaudient's final word, **Hamsuke?**

He wants me to ***stop*** training with you so I can concentrate on a more ***spiritual*** path to ninja mastery.

In short, I'll be **cleaning** the camp from here on out.

And Master Toga?

The same.

So, what are you going to do?

I have no choice!

They've taken ***everything*** from me.

No. You did this.
Everyone except you, Master.
You've always taught me to follow my own destiny.
I am in the minority.
And my hands are tied.
Your preoccupation with Shianndrea is going to get you kicked out of the clan altogether.
I warned you before.
Everyone that sits on the Council of Elders believes that girl to be our savior.
You have to fix this on your own.
One of the best I have ever trained.
You are simply over-shadowed by an antiquated belief that Shianndrea is the chosen one of our clan.
You are a fine ninja, Hamasuke.
I am sorry for that.
How can I fix this on my own, Master?
Destroy the belief.
PAGE 3

THE DOJO
Come on, Shianndrea! Keep up!
KIAH!
Good.
TURRA: AGE 18

HEY!!!
OOFF!
Eyes off the target?
Butt on the ground.
Besides, that's **gross**, the way you've been oogling my little brother, Shianndrea.
PAGE 5

Ow!
I wasn't **oogling**, Turra.
I mean... he—

—Sure. I've seen the big doe eyes when Kim mopes in.
I swear, I don't know what you see in him.
He's always so... **stale.**

He's not stale. He's just serious.
Seriously **HOT!!**
Geez! You guys are really making me wanana hurl right about now.
Did I hear you girls say my name?
CYAN: AGE 15

You did say "**hot,**" didn't you?
No, we were talking about hurling.
So your timing is perfect, Cyan.

All this style, grace, the winning smile.
It makes you nervous.
I get it.
Don't you guys think we make the perfect couple?
Ugh.

PAGE 6

Ahem! Shianndrea, Megumi...
I hope that your training is going well.
You both are looking stronger every day.
Kim!
So, what brings you to our reindeer games?
I have a mission.
Father has asked me to continue my surveillance of the Azumi ninja and ascertain Kokoro's plan of attack.

Ascertain? He sounds like our dad.

Heh. He's a 40 year old man in a 16 year old body.

So. I guess we're going to be pulling an **all nighter** on this stake out.

Care to **join us,** Turra?

Uh...

You're not going this time, Cyan.

Father wanted me to take **Shianndrea** on this mission.

Me? W - why?

Father thinks it's a good **idea** for you to learn from me in the **field** considering how well you did the other day.

I agree.

I mean... If you **agree,** that is.

I - I agree.

Well, since we're all in "**agreement**", can I get back to my training session now?

Megumi, you're up next.

Greeeat.

New Tokyo

I've been **staking** out this place for months.

Nearly everyone in there has either been in the **Yakuza** or is currently a part of it.

Yakuza. That's like the mob in America, right?

In a way.

But I thought we were looking for the Azumi.

The Azumi Clan are the Yakuza's **lap dogs.**

That's how they got their operational budget before they hooked up with Terminus.

With any luck, we will be able to find out what Kokoro has in store for us.

AI: AGE 18

Well, well.
This looks **cozy.**

Ai! Hey.
What are you doing here?
"What are you doing here?"
Is that any way to greet your girlfriend?
Girlfriend?
Besides, Master Gaudient suggested that I tag along.
He thought Shianndrea could learn something from me also.
Looks like everyone has a lesson for me today.
But I only planned for a two-person mission.
So, just change it.
God, you are stubborn sometimes.
Shianndrea, what's been going on?
Nothing now.
Hmm?
Nothing.
We were just staking out Ramen Delight in hopes...
Wait.
That's him.

It's Kokoro!

Looks like I was **right.**

Let's follow that truck.

They're stopping.

They've stopped?! What's he planning?

What?!

RAGHA!!

This...

isn't...

...good.

PERFECT!
Bring Shianndrea to me.
Kill the others.
Easier said than done, Mr. Hairy Back.
Shianndrea, on your feet!
I think it's time to show me some of those killer moves Kim has been bragging about.
On it!
Let's chop "Harry and the Hendersons" down!

PAGE 14

UNGAH!!

MASTER KOKORO, WE HAVE THE GIRL.

WATCH OUT!

SHIANNDREA!!

AI, PROTECT HER!

I... don't... need...

...PROTECTION!!

UMPHA!

GNATS! ALL OF YOU!
Woah!
Mr. Hairy Back looks like he's pretty upset!
Thoughts, Kim?
We're compromised and out num-bered!
We retreat.
For now.
Ever closer.
PAGE 16

KIM AND AI!?

When did this **happen** and why didn't I **know** about it?

I don't know.

Look, it's no big **deal**.

I'm the one that almost got **caught**, remember?

Oh yeah.

Geez. How stupid was I?

He could **never** have liked me **anyway**.

I mean, it's Ai.

Everyone **loves** her.

Yeah. Talk about competition.

Hey Turra, Shianndrea.

You were **awesome** last night, Shianndrea.

Thanks.

You should've seen her, Turra.

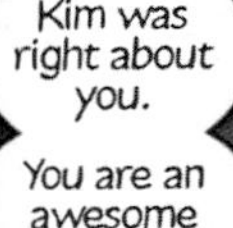

TO BE CONTINUED

SHIANNDREA BY JULES RIVERA

Shianndrea Toshigawa

Maybe if I put heels on these things. Yeah, I can see it now. "Shianndrea breaks her ankles while trying to side-kick." Jeez!
-Shianndrea

Since birth, Shianndrea Toshigawa has been told she was "special" by the Toshigawa Council of Elders. Her mentor, Master Gaudient, has even claimed to have seen her manifest great power when she was only a little girl. Shianndrea doesn't remember anything and she really doesn't believe a word of it. She only wants to be a normal girl and has fallen head-over-heels for her trainer, Kim Shibata. Because of her affections for Kim, and his apparent blindness to it, she is very self-conscious and tends to doubt her own abilities. However, her true skill and bravery always shows through in the end. Though her real abilities remain a mystery, her linage is all too clear. She is the direct descendant of the Toshigawa bloodline. She is also the daughter of the evil Emperor of Japan, making this Ninja Princess popular in the wrong way.

Megumi Goya

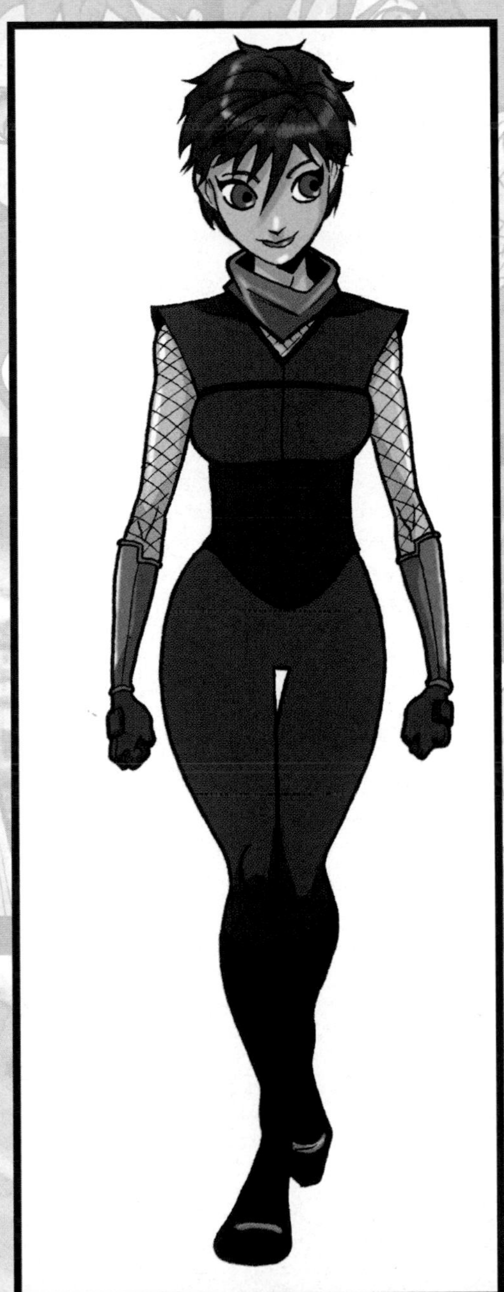

Wow. He said you were perfect.
That's the most praise
I've seen Kim give anyone.
-Megumi

If Shianndrea has a best friend, it's Megumi Goya. She is a loyal and good friend. Meek and very shy, Megumi and Shianndrea feed off of each other's confidence and can be seen whispering to each other in the corner about the guys that pass by. Megumi comes from a long line of Toshigawa supporters and has followed her lineage into the Toshigawa ninja ranks. However, her abilities are not what they should be. Although her ninja skill needs much work, her skills with throwing stars are almost unmatched. She often wishes she could leave the life of the ninja behind and pursue a life outside the clan. However, she couldn't do so without her best friend, Shianndrea.

You are coming with me, Shianndrea.

5 YEARS AGO

NO! YOU JUST CAN'T TAKE HER!

WHATEVER IS HAPPENING, YOU CAN'T FORCE HER TO BE A PART OF THIS!

WE HAVE TO TALK!

I have nothing to say to you.

Your betrayal is complete.

Shianndrea's destiny is MINE to mold.

SHINOBI

NINJA PRINCESS™

FREEFALL

Martheus Wade • Creator • Writer • Artist

Part Two

To me, Shianndrea. NOW!!
Please, Steven. You have to forgive me!
I didn't want to hurt you. I just missed you so much!
Please don't go!
Don't take her away from me.
Don't touch me.
Listen, my love. We can leave here.
The Council would never know where we've gone.
We can mend things and raise Shianddrea together.
Away from the fighting.
Mommy?!
Don't touch me.
Steven?

DON'T TOUCH ME!!!!

Gah! Humph!

MASTER? ARE YOU ALL RIGHT?

I'm fine. Do not **concern** yourself with my well being, Desai.

Get my daughter so that we end this.

The Toshigawa shall be ***no more.***

FREEFALL

TO BE CONTINUED

SHINOBI

NINJA PRINCESS™

3

Rekishi 歴史

NEXT ISSUE

IF BETTY AND VERONICA BROKE BAD...

NUTMEG

nutmeg 1/2 cup x3
salt 1/4 tsp
sugar 1 cup
flour 1/2 cup
butter 1/2 cup
eggs 2
cocoa powder 1/3 cup
baking powder 1/4 tsp
vanilla extract 1 tsp

bake at 350°!!

Poppy + cassia

COMING SOON!

ACTION LAB
TWO LABORATORY GROWN TEENS... LOST IN SPAC
H2012
PLANET GIGANTIC
OCTOBER 2014

THE WORLD'S MIGHTIEST HERO.

JAMIE DALLESSANDRO

1966 - 2014

ACTION
LAB
READ MORE NOW

Shinobi: Ninja Princess - Action Lab
www.actionlabcomics.com
00211
7 00465 77240 4

SHINOBI

NINJA PRINCESS™

3

Rekishi 歴史

Martheus Wade

Janet Wade

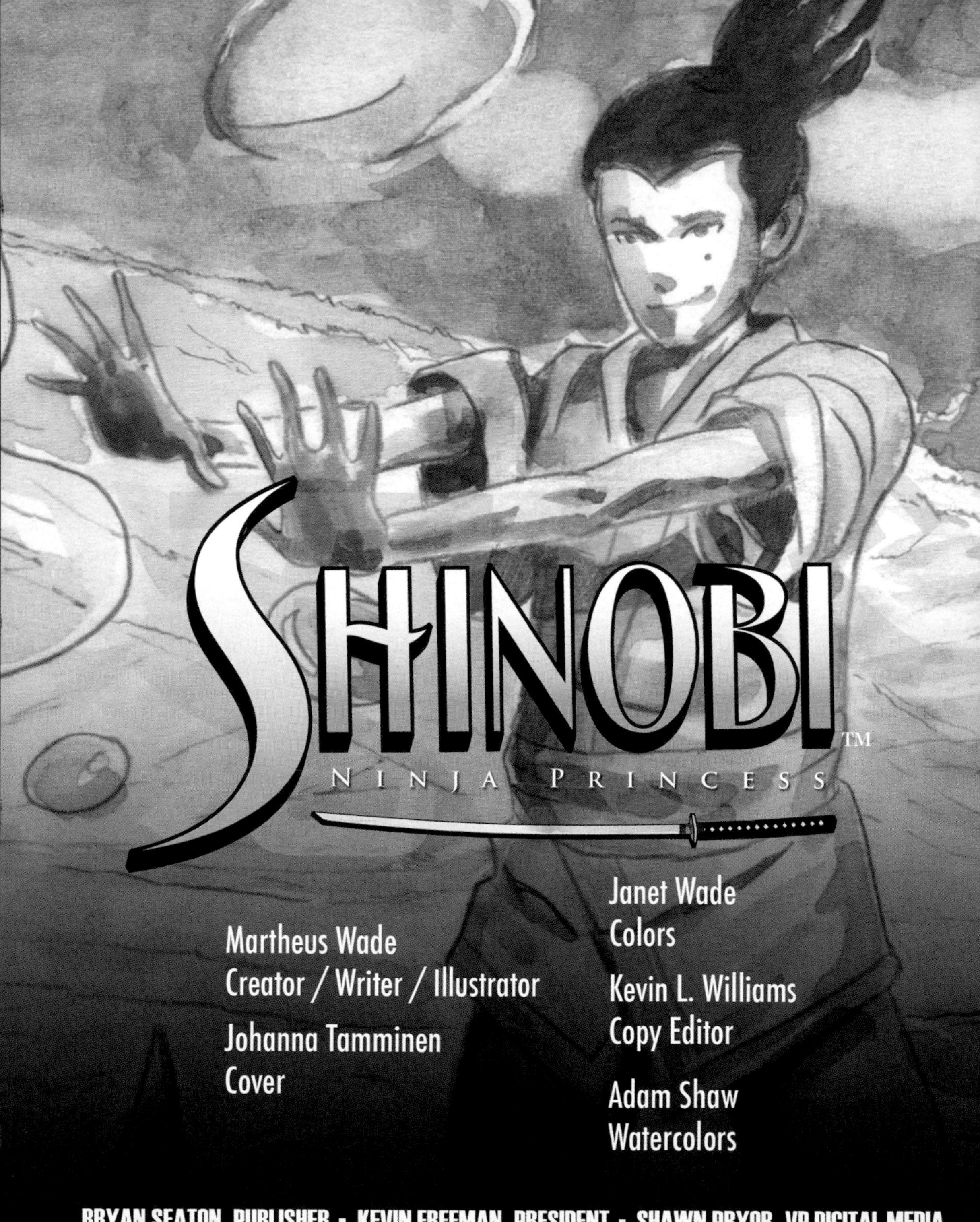

Martheus Wade
Creator / Writer / Illustrator

Johanna Tamminen
Cover

Janet Wade
Colors

Kevin L. Williams
Copy Editor

Adam Shaw
Watercolors

Shinobi: Ninja Princess 3, October 2014.
Published by Action Lab Entertainment. Printed in Canada. First Printing.

Action Lab

TOSHIGAWA HEADQUARTERS
THE HOME OF MASTER JUBEI
Good night, Kristen. Sweet dreams.
KRISTEN: AGE 10

Shianndrea?

PAGE 1

I'm surprised you are still **awake,** Shianndrea.

Master Jubei. I'm sorry. I- I just **can't** sleep.

Are you **worried** about your **Masters Test** in a few days?

It is a grueling physical and mental exam of your skills.

But I'm sure you are **ready,** my child.

No, it's not the test.

Everyone talks about this great power I have and how I am the savior of our clan.

But, I've never felt... **special**.

I don't even know what this "power" is.

I love training and the martial arts.

I'm good at it.

But what I really want...

What I really want just seems so far away.

Can I tell you a story, Shianndrea?

It's not **"The Ninja-ending Story"** again?

You told me that **supposed** "bedtime tale" when I was little.

I couldn't sleep for **weeks.**

No, not this time.

This is a story about your ancestor, Yamato Toshigawa.

Yamato was a young fisherman who lived in a small village on the outskirts of Edo. He loved to fish and made sure his village never went without food. However, he hid a great secret.

Yamato could move objects with his mind. He was so powerful that he could actually feel the fish swimming in the sea. It allowed him to make sure that his people would never go hungry. But, he guarded this secret with his life in fear of what his village would think of him.

Oh.

YAHHHH!!

Yamato, sprang into action and saved the woman before she drowned.

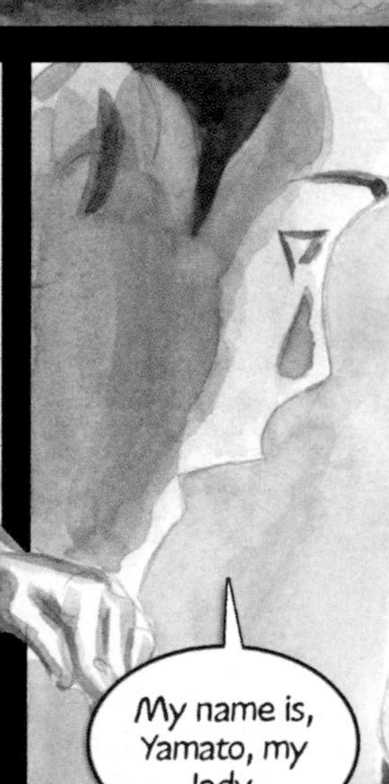
As he pulled her to the sandy beach, Yamato recognized the beautiful woman to be Tokuhime, the daughter of Nobunaga Oda, a powerful ruler.
She opened her eyes and it was love at first sight for the young fisherman.

You... you **saved me.**
Thank you, fisherman.
My name is, Yamato, my lady.

PAGE 4

However, Yamato knew that, because of who she was, she was promised to another man.
Still, he took the injured Tokuhime on the long journey back to his village to nurse her to health.
Unbeknownst to Yamato the demon lord Dagamon was deep in pursuit of the beautiful princess.
Why was this Dagamon after Tokuhime, Jubei?
The demon was summoned by her future mother-in-law to kill Tokuhime and prevent the union of two households.
When Yamato rescued Tokuhime, he became a great threat to her mother-in-law's evil plans.
A month passed, and both Yamato and Tokuhime grew very close.
Everywhere he went, she followed.
He became her protector and she became his confidant.
He even shared with her his greatest secret.
Yamato wanted nothing more than to be with Tokuhime.
However—
PAGE 5

How could a princess ever love a fisherman?

It's time you go back home, Tokuhime.

Seek the **protection** of your father.

You don't **belong** here.

We don't belong **together**.

That is where you are **wrong**.

I **belong** where my heart is and it's **here** with you, Yamato.

She did not care if he was a fisherman. She saw how special he was to his village and urged him to share his gift with them.

However, Dagamon's rage scorched the land. Villages burned in his search for the princess.
As happiness bloomed...
...death fell all around them.
As their world stood still...
... the rest of the world spun out of control.
PAGE 7

Wait. I thought this wasn't a ***horror story.***

Besides, the way you and the Council of Elders talk about Yamato Toshigawa...

...you'd think he was a ***super man*** or something.

How could the founder of our clan, allow Damgamon to hurt **innocent people**?

Good question. The Yamato in this story was a different man.

Aw man! Look at this catch. Not enough here to even feed the **village cat.**

That bad, huh?

Yeah. It's just not my day for fishing.

Good!

Maybe you can just go and **explain** things to the village?

You know, you could say, "Well, you see guys. My ***powers*** weren't working and all."

I'm sure they would **understand.**

Oh you're "***sure***", right?

And I'm "***sure***" this is one of your plots to get me to **come clean.**

Would I do a thing like that?!

YES!!!

HAHAHAHA!!!!

HAHAHAHA!!!!

HAHAHAHA!!!!

HAHAHAHA!!!!

HAHAHAHA!!!!

BOOM
OH NO!

THE VILLAGE!!

No! The Oni. He's found me!

PAGE 10

TOKUHIME!
YOUR DEATH IS AT HAND!
Dagamon found the princess.
Yamato watched in horror as Dagamon burned houses and struck down villagers like lightning.

BEGONE FISHERMAN.
UNGHA!!
YAMATO!!

I'm - I'm fine.
Tokuhime! You've got to get out of here!
There - there is no time. He will kill everyone.

In the fury and flame, Tokuhime took Yamato's hand and whispered in his ear -

Now is the time, my love.

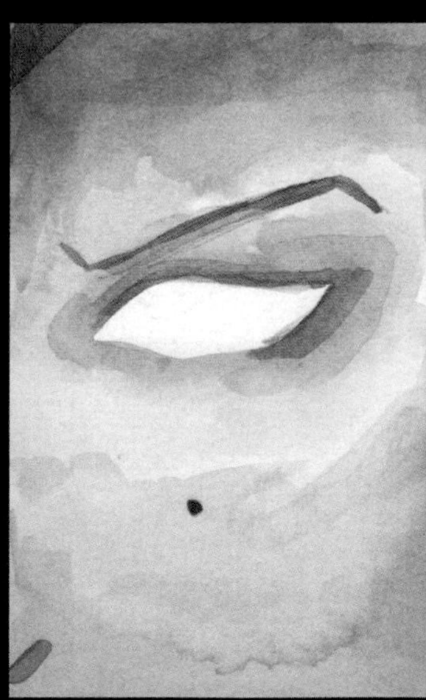

GET DOWN!

Yamato unleashed a furious attack that took Dagamon off guard.

With his great power,
he defeated Dagamon.

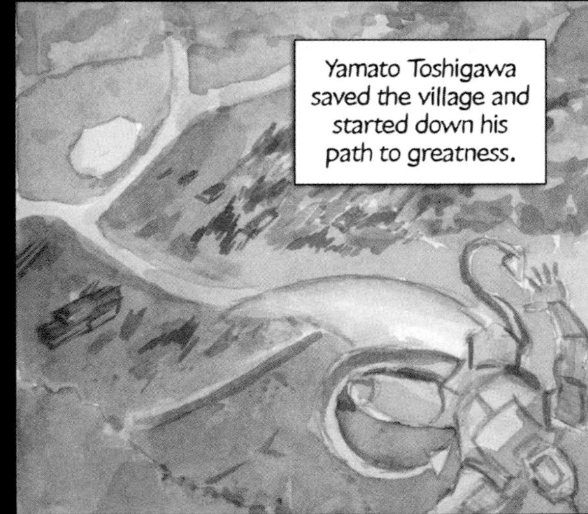

And he and Tokuhime lived **happily ever after.**
Not quite.
What?! But Yamato **defeated** Dagamon.
Tokuhime knew that she had to **return** to her home to end her mother-in-law's **treachery.**
But that would mean she would have to marry **someone else.**
That is right.
Both **Yamato** and **Tokuhime** agreed that she would return to her home, unify the families, and bring an end to the conflict.
With a kiss, Tokuhime rode into the sunset toward her village, vowing to return to Yamato **someday.**
This is **worse** than "The Ninja-ending Story".
I **thought** you were going to make me feel **better.**
You are like my daughter, **Shianndrea.**
I have seen how you **look** at Kim.
You two have been close since you were very young.
And yet, you have **never** let him see who you **really** are.

When Tokuhime saw who Yamato **truly was**, it did not matter **what** he was.

All that mattered was what was in his **heart**.

Because he allowed himself to be, well, **himself**, he saved not only his people, but countless **others**.

He **became** a hero and rose to create our ninja clan.

He fulfilled his destiny.

Be your **remarkable self**, Shianndrea and everyone will take notice.

Even Kim.

Thank you, Master Jubei.

Alright. Off to bed with you.

You have busy days ahead of you.

Don't remind me.

You will do fine, my child.

Master, did Tokuhime ever **return** to Yamato?

That is a story for **another** time.

She did.

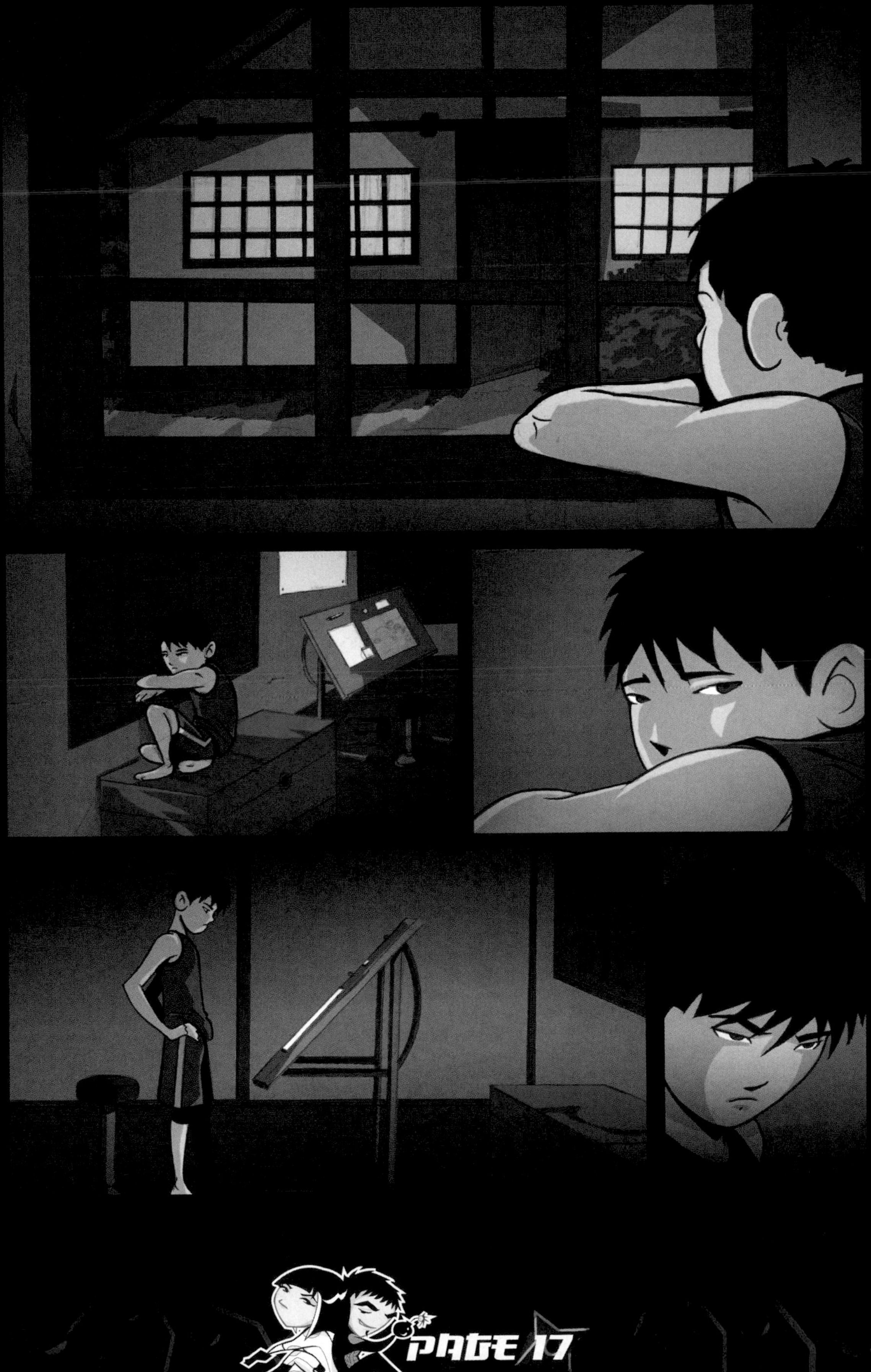

PAGE 17

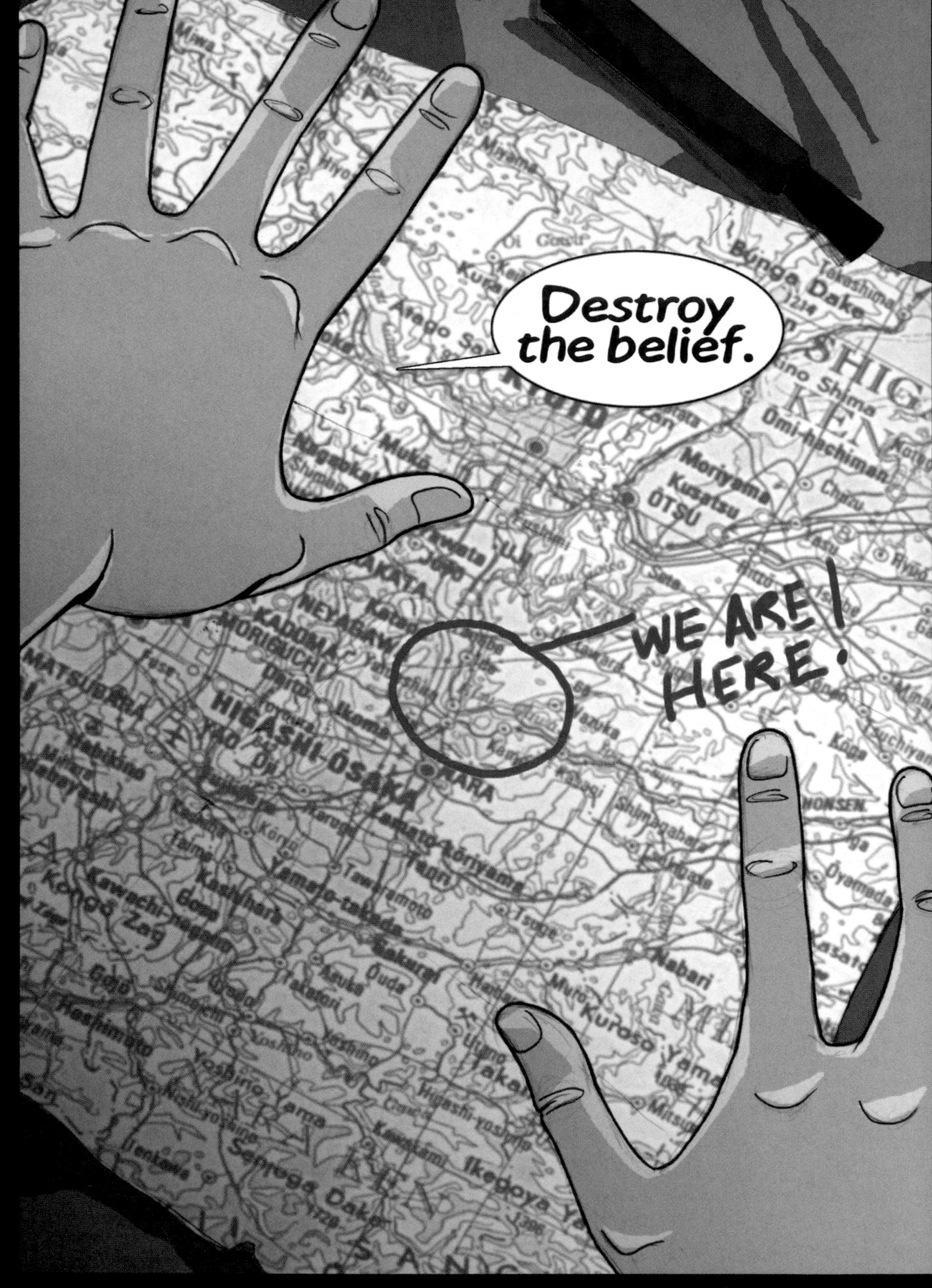

TO BE CONTINUED

ONI BY JUSTIN STEWART

Kim Shibata

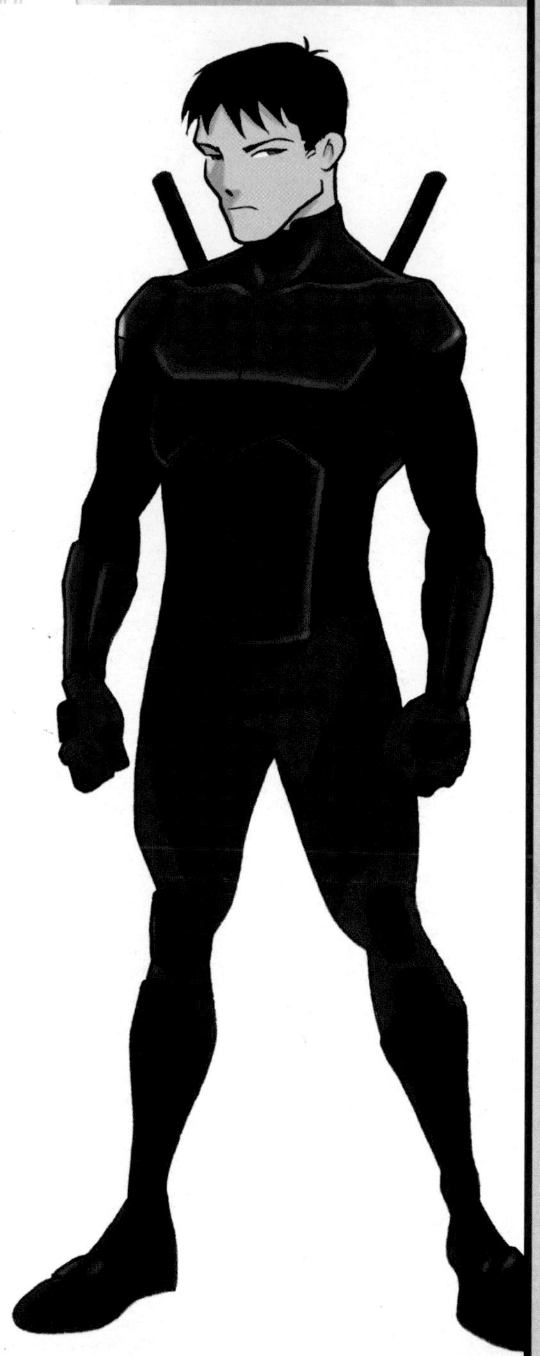

This will be no easy task. I have fought this Oni before and he is nearly indestructible. Our only hope is to contain him in some way. When I call your name, please step forward.
-Kim

Kim Shibata is the definition of a handsome duty-bound warrior. He is the trainer of the younger Toshigawa ninja who are on the verge of attaining the rank of Master. His father, Gaudient, trusts his abilities beyond any other. He is the first one The Council of Elders call upon to lead important missions.

A master ninja himself, he takes his responsibilities as a leader very seriously and training is his life. Every girl in the clan wants to call him their boyfriend. Although he is the most sought after ninja in the clan, Kim is awkward around girls. His awkwardness only adds to his appeal, however, and he has caught the eye of one of the most popular girls in the clan, Ai Ishikawa. Being in a relationship with Ai is a big change for Kim and he is working hard to "come out of his shell."

Ai Ishikawa

Boyish?! I know he's not talking about me. So he's got to be talking about you, Shianndrea.
-Ai

Ai Ishikawa is loved by everyone. She's stylish, beautiful and very confident. Her winning smile and ninja skill are able to win over the Council of Elders as well as warm Gaudient's cold stare. Every guy wants to get to know her and every girl wants to be her, even Shianndrea. Even though she is aware of her charm, Ai is one of the nicest ninja in the Toshigawa clan and can make light of any situation.

However, she is also one of the most skilled. She is a master ninja and her combat abilities allowed Kim to fall for her despite himself. Ai is deeply in love with Kim as well and values his companionship over anything else. Through Kim's constant bragging of Shianndrea's skill, Ai sees a kindred spirit in the young ninja. Despite their mutual interest in Kim, Ai and Shianndrea become friends.

5 Years Ago

MOMMY!! OH... OH NO!!

UNGHA!

SHINOBI
NINJA PRINCESS™

FREEFALL Part Three

Martheus Wade • Creator • Writer • Artist

SHIANNDREA TOSHIGAWA!!
Please... Mommy! Wake up!
WAKE UP!
YOU CANNOT HIDE FROM ME!
YOUR MOTHER IS DEAD!!
YOU WILL COME WITH ME.
MASTER TERMINUS DEEMS IT SO.
MOMMY!

STEP AWAY FROM THEM!!
YOUR DESTRUCTIVE RAMPAGE ENDS NOW, MONSTER!
GAUDIENT. TAKI SATO.
YOU CONTINUE TO FIGHT IN THE FACE OF YOUR DESTRUCTION.
THAT IS ADMIRABLE AND FUTILE.
GAUDIENT!! HELP ME!!!

He's... He's too **strong** for them.

They **can't** win!

Why did you do this to us, Daddy?

GAUDIENT!!!

DON'T LEAVE ME!!

ARRGHA!! KUMIKO!!! SHIANNDREA!!

FREEFALL

TO BE CONTINUED

SHINOBI

NINJA PRINCESS™

4

Oni 鬼

NEXT ISSUE

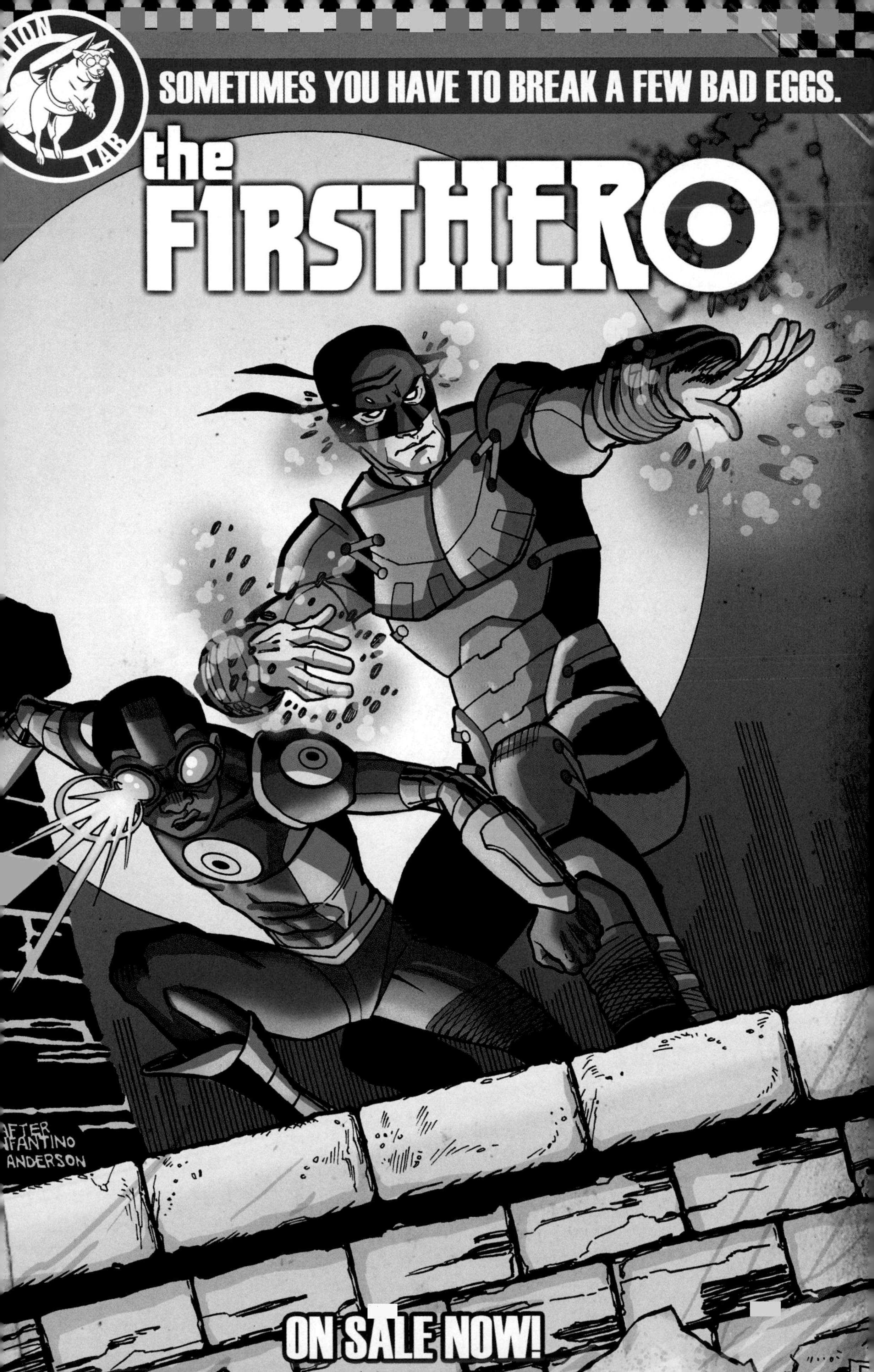

ACTION LAB
NEW FRIENDS. NEW ENEMIES. NEW ADVENTUR
Princeless
COMING SOON

TO SAVE HER BROTHER, SHE WILL BECOME A HERO.
FIGHT LIKE A GIRL
NOVEMBER 2014

ACTION
LAB

ACTION LAB
SHINOBI
NINJA PRINCESS ™
4
Oni 鬼
Martheus Wade
Janet Wade
bi: Ninja Princess - Action Lab
actionlabcomics.com
00411
00465 77240 4

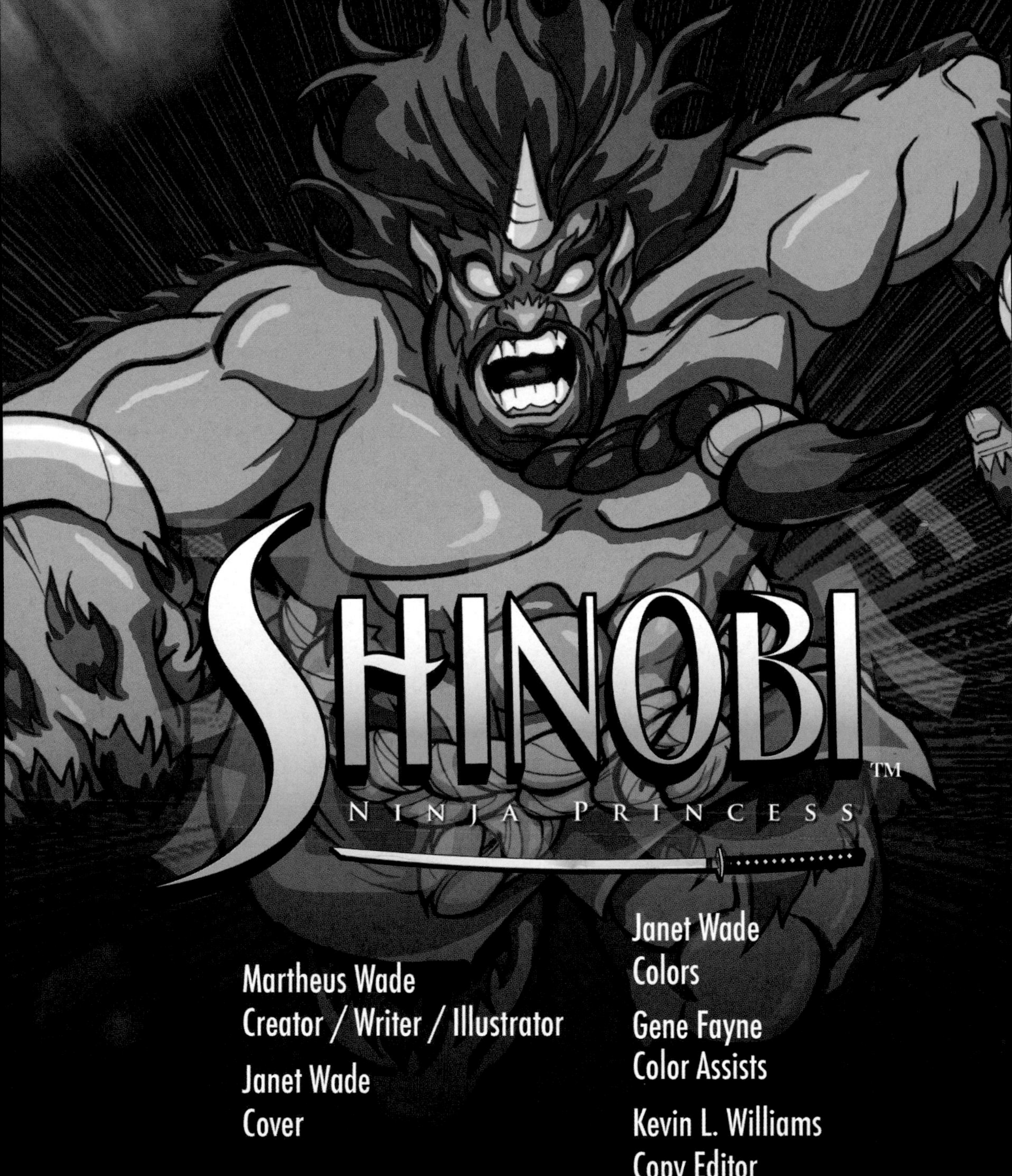

Martheus Wade
Creator / Writer / Illustrator

Janet Wade
Cover

Janet Wade
Colors

Gene Fayne
Color Assists

Kevin L. Williams
Copy Editor

BRYAN SEATON- PUBLISHER • KEVIN FREEMAN- PRESIDENT • SHAWN PRYOR- VP DIGITAL MEDIA
DAVE DWONCH- CREATIVE DIRECTOR • SHAWN GABBORIN- EDITOR IN CHIEF
JAMAL IGLE & KELLY DALE- CO-DIRECTORS OF MARKETING
JEREMY WHITLEY- EDUCATION OUTREACH DIRECTOR
CHAD CICCONI- SECRETLY "THE DANDELION"

SMALL TOSHIGAWA OUTPOST
EARLY MORNING

HUH?

WHUMP!
WHUMP!
WHUMP!

CRASH

GAH!!

OH...
OH NO!!

ROAR!!!

NO! STOP!!
NO.
NOT UNTIL YOU DO SOMETHING FOR ME.
Do something? For you?
CALL THEM!
CALL THEM ALL!
PAGE 3

TOSHIGAWA NINJA CAMP

SHIANNDREA'S ROOM

Ugha!

If only I could get one night of **good sleep.**

I could get rid of these **bags** under my eyes.

No wonder Kim **never** really noticed **me.**

YAWN!

Ai's gorgeous I'm a **hot mess.**

Maybe I can **blame** my uniform for making me look like a **boy?**

SNIFF! SNIFF!

HUH?!

Kim?
Ai?
Come on, Slow Poke. KEEP UP.

Hamasuke! What's going on?
I don't know.
There was a high alert and Master Gaudient called everyone to the dojo for briefing.
You're not going?
No.
I'm sorry, Hamasuke. I didn't know that... I didn't want--
--I'd like to finish sweeping before nightfall, this time.
Here you are!
I was just coming to get you but you weren't in your room!
Let's go!
We're late as is!

This is the last footage from our southern security outpost near Kobe.
They are under attack by, what looks to be, the Oni associated with the Azumi Ninja clan.
If left unchecked, he could wipe out the entire southern outpost.
Oni?
Your mission will be to aid our brothers and sisters in warding off this demon.
Isn't that "Harry", the monster we fought in New Tokyo a few nights ago?
Yes. The Azumi have been tampering with some sort of mystic arts.
Whatever they have been doing, it is why we could not so much as scratch him before.

Kim will select his strike team for this assign-ment.
This will be no easy task.
I have fought this Oni before and he is nearly indestructible.
Our only hope is to contain him in some way.
When I call your name, please step forward.
Turra.
Great. First name on the list.
Oh joy.
Cyan.
That's right.
Ai.
It's a date, then.
Hana.
Tanji.
Kin.
Shianndrea.
Kim, I have a slight change to your strike team that I need for you to consider.
The Council and myself agree that this could be a trap, an elaborate set-up in order to draw Shianndrea out into the open.
I would like Megumi to take Shianndrea's place on the strike team.
Furthermore, Ai should stay behind to stand guard while the majority are away.

But... You can't break up **the team.**

The Council has spoken.

Megumi, you will **replace** Shianndrea.

Ai, you will stand guard and protect Shianndrea.

This blows! Come on, Shianndrea.

Toshigawa! Disperse!

You said that we were all in agreement.
However, was it wise to separate Shianndrea from Kim?
He is her direct trainer.
As well, Kim and Ai are currently in a relationship.
This could cause problems between two of our most gifted masters.
I understand your concerns, my Masters.
But those are the exact reasons I had to step in.
I've seen the way my son... acts when he is around Shianndrea.
At the same time, his relationship with Ai has a tendency to impair his judgement.
It is better for him to concentrate on his assignment, rather than his conflicting emotions.
I can't believe Kim!
I can't believe he chose duty over me!
Well, it really wasn't Kim's fault.
Gaudient was the one who changed everything.
Still. Kim could have stood up for me.
I haven't been on guard duty since I was 12.
What's he trying to pull?
We're not taking this lying down, Shianndrea.
Come on!
Where are we going?
We're going to help Kim.
PAGE 10

YARGA!!

POW! POW!!

POW! POW!!

CYAN!! Grab Tanji!!

OOFF!

Tanji! You alright, man?

Yeah.

What's that thing **made of?**

I don't know.

But it's kicking our butts!

Megumi, hold on!
GNATS!!
ALL OF YOU ARE NOTHING TO ME!!
RARGHA!! YOU!!
KIM!!
YOU WILL BRING ME THE BOYISH GIRL!
Boyish?!
I know he's not talking about me.
PAGE 13

So he's **got** to be talking about **you**, Shianndrea.
Don't **remind** me, ok.
What are you two doing here?!?
It looks like we're ***saving you.***
ARRGHA!!

"Thanks, babe, for **saving** my life."
Typical.
You **shouldn't** be here.
Shianndrea shouldn't be here.

Wait. What are you doing?!
You can't--
I'm just as good as **she is**, Kim!

I can **handle** this!
Turra!
Pressure him and keep his attention away from Shianndrea and Ai.
ON IT!

Tanji, Hana,
Megumi, Kin.
Hit him low. Keep him off balance.

ATTACK!!

KIAH!

BOOM!!!

Wow!

ARRGAH!!

What?

No!
GRAB!

NO!

AHHHH!!

Shianndrea!!!
NO!
Uh...
Hi?

PAGE 19

LATER
It's just a little sore, Turra.
I'm fine.
You may be.
But I wonder will they.
What were you thinking, Ai?
Shianndrea could have been killed.
You always pick what your father says over what you know is right, Kim.
I should've been on that mission to begin with.
So you endanger Shianndrea just to make a point?
Why is this all about her?
She's fine.
We aren't.

The Oni was **successful** in his attack on the Toshigawa outpost in Kobe.

However, he was **defeated** before he could bring back our **prize.**

TO BE CONTINUED

HAMASUKE FALLING
BY JANET WADE

Turra Shibata

Sure. I've seen the big doe eyes when Kim mopes in. I swear I don't know what you see in him. He's always so... stale.
-Turra

Turra Shibata is Kim's older sister and the two couldn't be more different. Where Kim embraces responsibility, Turra turns her back on it, wanting to concentrate on having fun rather than training.

Still, her carefree attitude doesn't diminish the skilled ninja she is. Turra is also a master ninja and uses her skill to teach the younger warriors the fine art of the katana sword. She is a fan of western culture and has incorporated a hand gun into her arsenal of ninja weapons. She has also expressed her personal style by dying her naturally black hair with platinum blonde streaks, much to her father, Gaudient's, disapproval. Because of her carefree life, Shianndrea looks up to Turra and aspires to be more like her.

Hamasuke Gozan

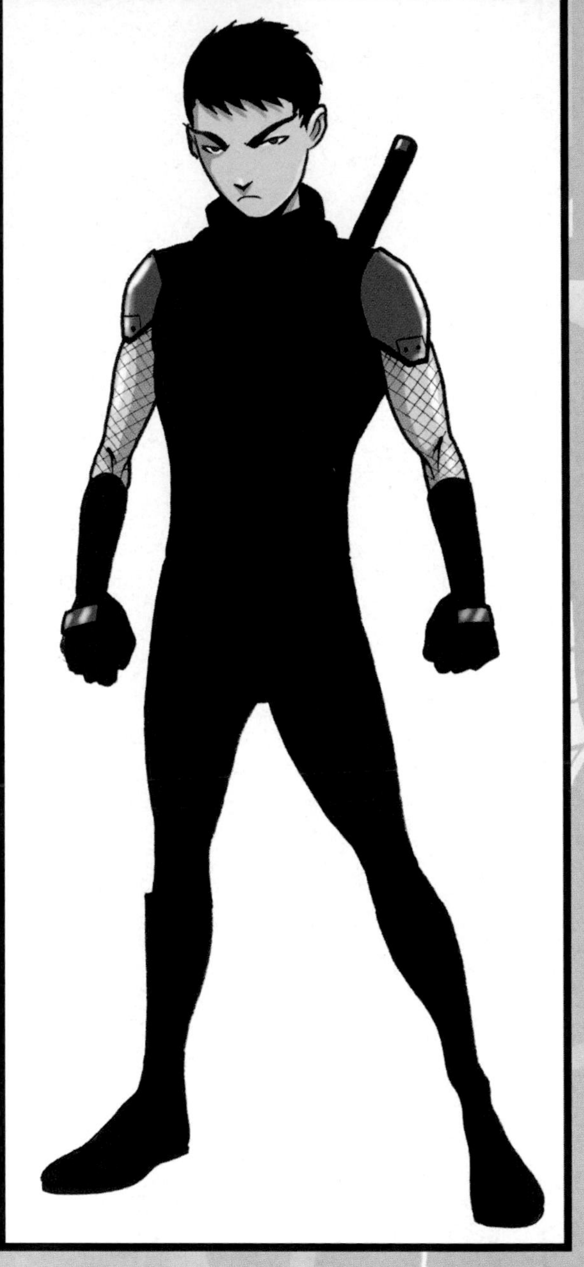

Both of you need to follow MY lead. Just stay here, keep the bench warm for me and stay out of my way. That's what kunoichi do best anyway.
-Hamasuke

Hamasuke Gozan is the ninja with a chip on his shoulder. He feels he has a lot to prove and a short time to do it in. While all of the other guys look up to Kim, Hamasuke despises him and longs to take his place as the dominant ninja in the clan. He is a skilled warrior. However, he feels his potential is stifled by the amount of attention Shianndrea gets from the other Masters. His jealousy fuels his rage and he often watches her from the shadows. His direct teacher, Master Ryuichi, has warned him that his fixation on Shianndrea will eventually lead him to ruin. But his true feelings hide a deep secret that could spell the end for Shianndrea if not kept in check.

5 Years Ago
DON'T LEAVE ME!!!
FREEFALL

THIS LIFE WILL BE A MEMORY.
YOU WILL SOON FIND YOUR PLACE BESIDE THE EMPEROR PARAMOUNT.
AND THIS WORLD MUNDANE.
MOMMY!! MOMMY WAKE UP!!
TIME TO GO.
EMPEROR TERMINUS IS WAITING.
Somebody Help me.
HELP ME!!

MORNING
Dreams.
Pant! Pant!
More dreams.
Pant! Pant!
Pant! Pant!
Pant! Pant!
More nightmares.

TOSHIGAWA NINJA CAMP
SHIANNDREA'S ROOM
Ugha!
If only I could get one night of good sleep.
I could get rid of these bags under my eyes.
No wonder Kim never really noticed me.
YAWN!
Ai's gorgeous I'm a hot mess.
Maybe I can blame my uniform for making me look like a boy?
SNIFF! SNIFF!
HUH?!
FREEFALL
THE BEGINNING

ACTION
LAB
SHINOBI
NINJA PRINCESS
TM
5
Tesuto テスト
NEXT ISSUE
Wade

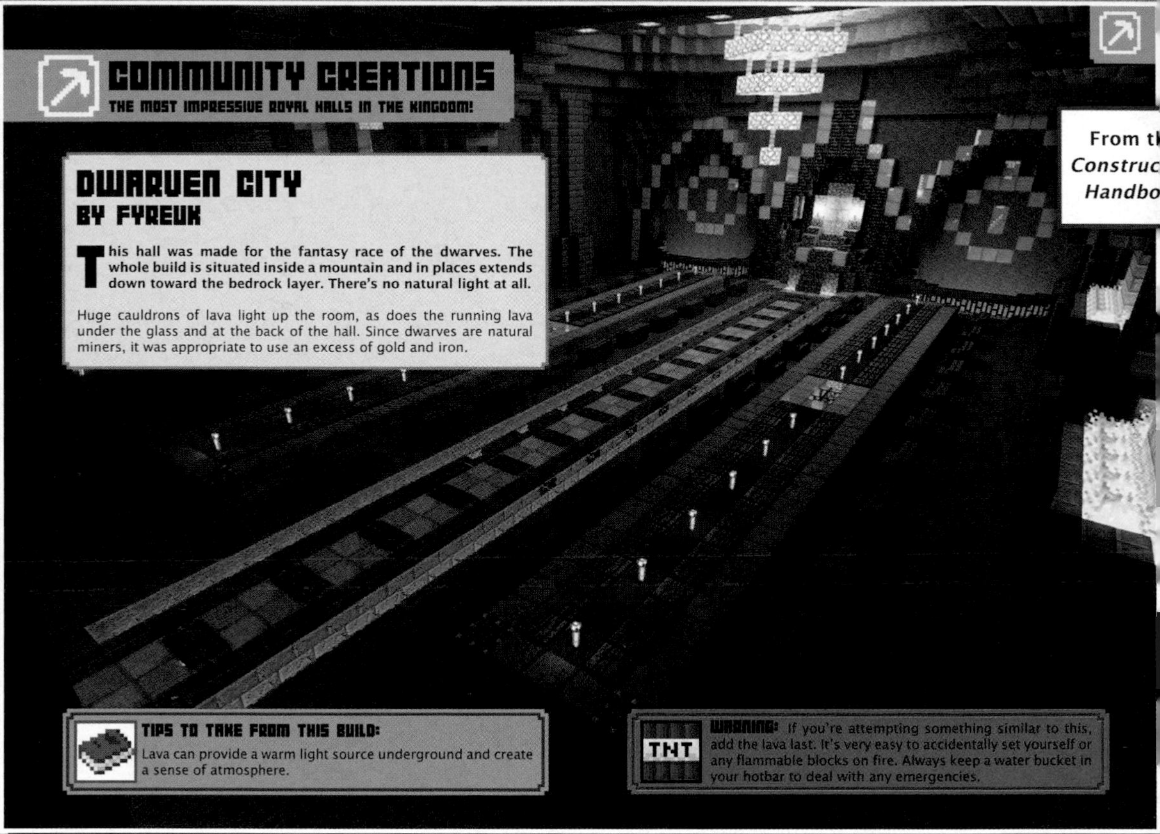

ACTION LAB
SHINOBI
NINJA PRINCESS
TM
5
Tesuto テスト
Martheus Wade
Janet Wade
Shinobi: Ninja Princess - Action Lab
www.actionlabcomics.com
00511
7 00465 77240 4

Martheus Wade
Creator / Writer / Illustrator

Gene Fayne
Colors

Tressina Bowling
Cover

Kevin L. Williams
Copy Editor

BRYAN SEATON- PUBLISHER • KEVIN FREEMAN- PRESIDENT • SHAWN PRYOR- VP DIGITAL MEDIA
DAVE DWONCH- CREATIVE DIRECTOR • SHAWN GABBORIN- EDITOR IN CHIEF
JAMAL IGLE & KELLY DALE- CO-DIRECTORS OF MARKETING
JEREMY WHITLEY- EDUCATION OUTREACH DIRECTOR
CHAD CICCONI- SECRETLY "THE DANDELION"

ACTION LAB

CHAMBER OF THE ELDERS

TOSHIGAWA HOLD

MASTERS TEST

Shianndrea Toshigawa, heir to the legacy of Yamoto Toshigawa and **Princess** of the **Toshigawa Ninja Clan.**

There are enemies at every turn.
As princess of our clan, you will be their main target.
However, it is most important that we do not hinder you from obtaining your destiny as a warrior and protector.
Do you accept this responsibility should you pass this test?
CLINK!
I do.
Then we shall begin.
PAGE 2

HAJIME!!

Wha!?!

SLASH!!

UMPH!

GET OVER HERE!

SLICE

SHING!!!

CLANG!!

SMACK!!!!

I've got to put some distance between me and them!

Halt!
Who goes there?

Heh!

YAH!!!

ALRIGHT!

You've **got** this Shianndrea!

Thanks guys!!

Good. But your test is **far from over.**

YES! THIS CONTEST IS FAR FROM OVER!

OH NO! THE AZUMI!!

GRRRRRR!!!!
CRASH!
HOW? We defeated you!!
TIME TO RETURN THE FAVOR.
It's Mr. Woolly Wonka and the Oompa Loompas!
I thought his name was Harry Hairy Back?
ATTACK!!
FINE!! I'LL JUST PUT YOU DOWN AGAIN!!!
NOT THIS TIME, GIRL!
THIS TIME YOU COME WITH US!
Shianndrea!
BACK, YOU BEAST!!
UH!

HMPH!

THERE SHE IS!
GET HER!!

NO!

OMPH!

ACK!!

RAGHA!!

ASAH!!

PAGE 9

GET OUT!!
My home has been burned down before.
IT WON'T HAPPEN AGAIN.
uhh...

PUSH THEM BACK!

WE MUST HOLD THEM UNTIL REINFORCEMENTS ARRIVE!

Wait.

OH NO!

SHIANNDREA!

SHIANNDREA!
SHIANNDREA!
SHIANNDREA!

We must get you out of here and to **safety.**
I order you to leave the fighting to us!
Master!
I can't **leave--**
GO!!

Oh.
Our home!

Everything is **destroyed.**
It's like when my mother **died.**

BOOM!

UNGHA!!

PAGE 13

All this trouble over a little girl.
Sure, you are a gifted ninja.
I'll give you that.
But all of this **death** and **destruction?**
If it weren't for ***you***, our two clans could probably coexist without so much as a **skirmish.**
However, as it is, you are the only thing standing in my way and the survival of **the Azumi.**
W-Why?
Because of who ***you are.***
The Emperor has paid us **handsomely** for your return.
He has also given favor to us if we bring you in.
We'd never have to worry about where our next assignment is going to come from.
Or if our children will have a decent meal at night.
Our lives will be set.
FOREVER!
Your people starve.
My people die.
All because of me.
Your time is ***over***, Toshigawa.
The Azumi ninja will rule.
Now and forever.

YARGA!!

This ends **now!**

You won't be taking her **anywhere,** Kokoro.

I get it now.
You're the ninja that broke into my office before.
I'm guessing you stole my map and graciously returned it the other day, pinpointing the Toshigawa camp's location.
Haha!!
I should thank you.
But tell me.
Why?
Why give us your location and then try to save her when we get here?
Haha! It makes no sense.
Ok. What do I have to lose?
I love her.
She has always had her eye on another.
In an effort to... impress her, I broke into your office against the wishes of my Masters.
I was punished.
The Masters took everything from me.
HAHA HA!
This is even better than I imagined.
Let me guess.
By staging all of this and saving the day, you hope to win the girl and get back into the good graces of the powers that be?
She's a PRINCESS, boy.
What could she possibly see in someone like you?
NO ONE LAUGHS AT ME!!
I AM HAMASUKE OF THE TOSHIGAWA NINJA!!
YOU WILL HONOR THAT!!!
PAGE 16

Heh!
GAH!!

PAGE 17

GEEZ!
You better be worth all of this trouble, girl.

POOM!
POOM!
POOM!
POOM!
POOM!

POOM!
POOM!

POOM!
POOM! POOM!

They are leaving.

I win.

After them!

Wait. Oh no.

Shianndrea!

Hamasuke!

Cyan, get Master Yuuka over here **now!!**

He must have tried to **defend** Shianndrea **alone.**

We lost.

That means they have her.

AZUMI NINJA CAMP

UNDERGROUND HOLDING CELL

Inform the Emperor that we have his daughter. We will be ready for him when he arrives.

TO BE CONTINUED

SHINOBI
NINJA PRINCESS
MEGUMI BY GREG CRAVENS

The World of the Shinobi

This is the first time you have been to New Tokyo, isn't it?
-Kim

The world is an untrusting place after World War III. Japan suffered greatly in the war and Tokyo was destroyed. The country was devastated. After the war, Terminus took control of the country and made Japan a financial power once again by creating Mecha that were used anywhere from domestic labor to military use. Through his new found popularity as a proficient leader, Emperor Terminus closed off the borders to Japan. He then restructured Japan and rebuilt Tokyo. Under his rule, Japan is divided into many different provinces. These provinces are ruled by generals in his Army. The generals answer only to Terminus, allowing him to micro-manage the country and search for his daughter, Shianndrea Toshigawa.

Because of this, there are only two ninja clans left: the Azumi Ninja Clan and the Toshigawa Ninja Clan. Though hunted by the new government and thriving in secret, the Toshigawa are the richer of the two clans due to the cultivation of various ancient financial contracts.

The Azumi, being the younger and poorer of the two clans, have had to scrap for contracts to get by. Their major contractor has been the Yakuza. It is the dream of Kokoro, head of the Azumi Ninja, to be free of the Yakuza's hold.

The two clans have been at odds for years as the Azumi Ninja strive to be in the Emperor's favor. They will do anything, even tamper with dark magic, to see this end a reality.

ACTION LAB
SHINOBI
6
Tesuto 2 テスト2
NEXT ISSUE
wade

ACTION LAB
TWO LABORATORY GROWN TEENS... LOST IN SPAC
PLANET GIGANTIC
H2012
ON SALE NOW!

TO SAVE HER BROTHER, SHE WILL BECOME A HERO.
FIGHT LIKE A GIRL
ON SALE NOW!

ACTION LAB
Princeless
COMING SOON

MINECRAFT™

The official handbooks packed with guides, exclusive interviews and tips from experts!

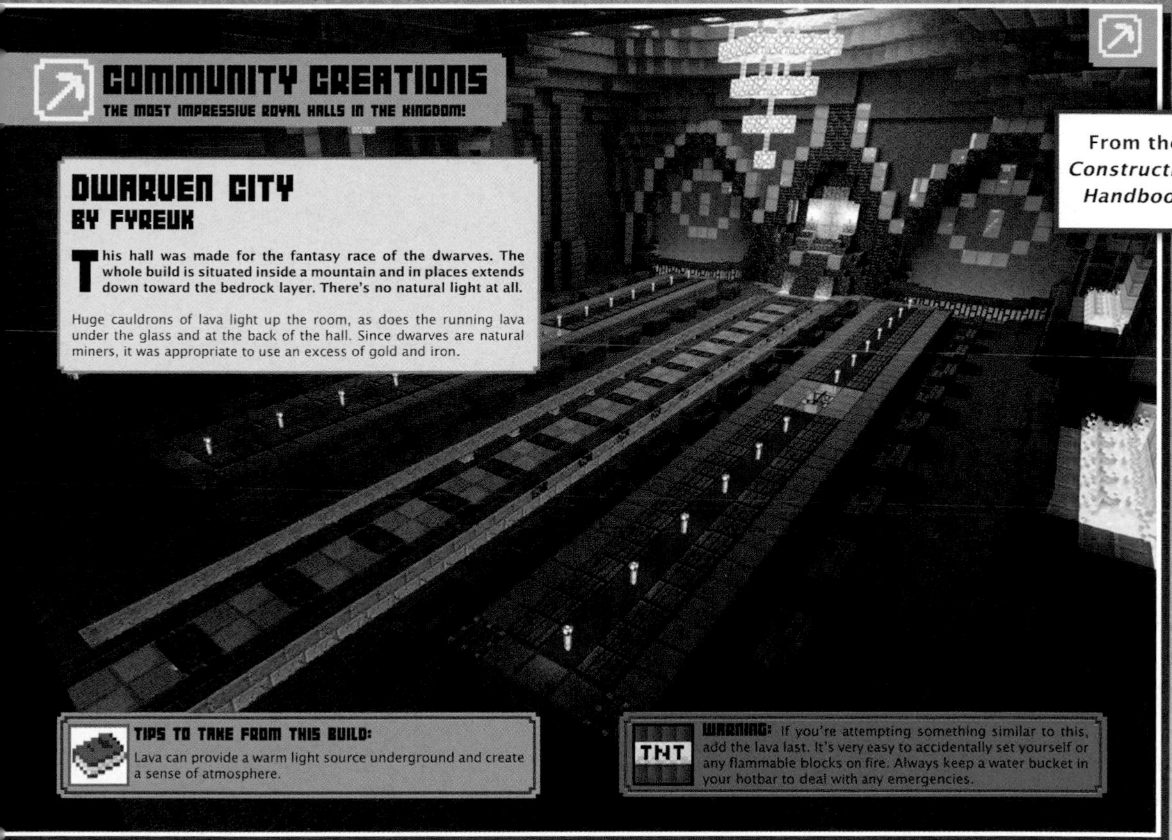

COMMUNITY CREATIONS

THE MOST IMPRESSIVE ROYAL HALLS IN THE KINGDOM!

From the *Construction Handbook*

DWARVEN CITY
BY FYREUK

This hall was made for the fantasy race of the dwarves. The whole build is situated inside a mountain and in places extends down toward the bedrock layer. There's no natural light at all.

Huge cauldrons of lava light up the room, as does the running lava under the glass and at the back of the hall. Since dwarves are natural miners, it was appropriate to use an excess of gold and iron.

TIPS TO TAKE FROM THIS BUILD: Lava can provide a warm light source underground and create a sense of atmosphere.

TNT **WARNING:** If you're attempting something similar to this, add the lava last. It's very easy to accidentally set yourself or any flammable blocks on fire. Always keep a water bucket in your hotbar to deal with any emergencies.

Includes All Four Handbooks!

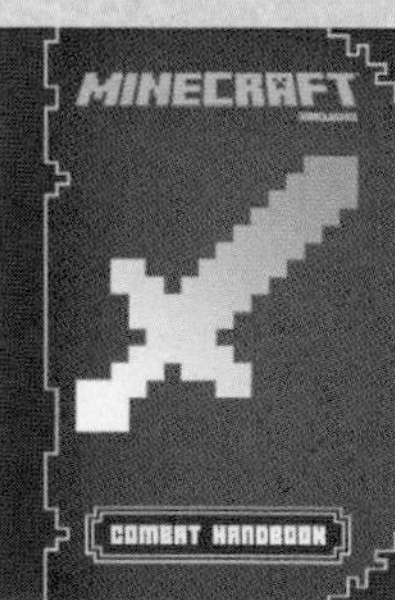

For more tips, visit SCHOLASTIC.COM/MINECRAFT

SCHOLASTIC
open a world of possible

ACTION LAB
SHINOBI
6
Tesuto 2 テスト2
Martheus Wade
Janet Wade
nobi: Ninja Princess - Action Lab
w.actionlabcomics.com
00611
00465 77240 4

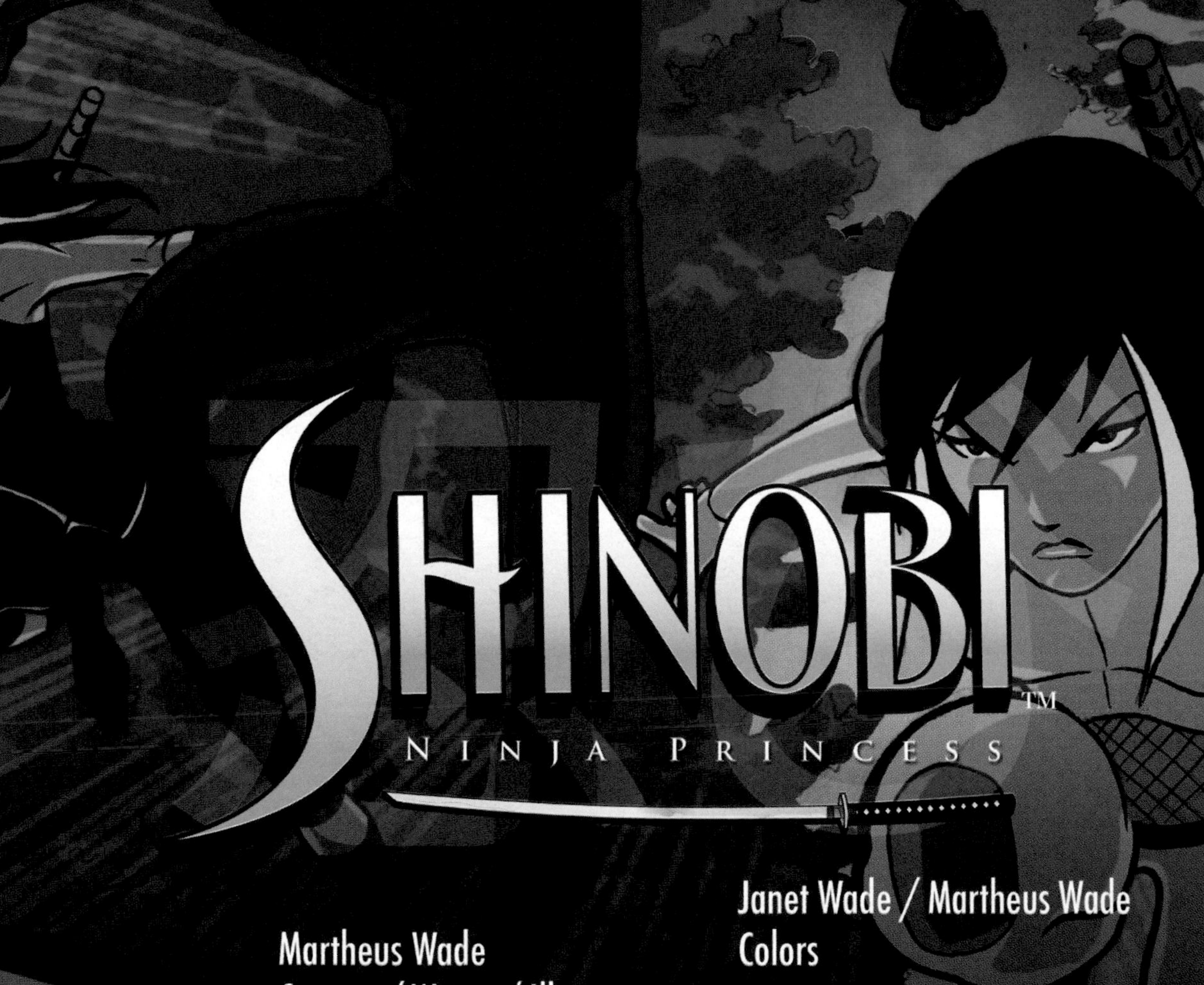

Martheus Wade
Creator / Writer / Illustrator

Martheus Wade
Cover

Janet Wade / Martheus Wade
Colors

Gene Fayne
Colors Assists

Kevin L. Williams
Copy Editor

BRYAN SEATON- PUBLISHER • KEVIN FREEMAN- PRESIDENT • SHAWN PRYOR- VP DIGITAL MEDIA
DAVE DWONCH- CREATIVE DIRECTOR • SHAWN GABBORIN- EDITOR IN CHIEF
JAMAL IGLE & KELLY DALE- CO-DIRECTORS OF MARKETING
JEREMY WHITLEY- EDUCATION OUTREACH DIRECTOR
CHAD CICCONI- SECRETLY "THE DANDELION"

ACTION LAB

THE TOSHIGAWA STRONGHOLD
What are we waiting for?
I'm not having Shianndrea sit there while we debate.
Besides, I want to give Kokoro a few more holes to--
--There is no question that we will go after her.
However, we need a plan.
Kokoro knows we will be coming for her.
So this will certainly be a trap.
And if the Emperor is in route to claim her, we could be facing his entire army as well.
Those are over-whelming odds, even for us.
PAGE 1

What's this all about?
Why does the **Emperor** want her so badly?
Centuries ago, **Yamato Toshigawa** defeated a great darkness, an Oni, that threatened to engulf the world.
Afterwards, he established our clan in hopes that we would protect the world.
In doing so, he foretold of one from his **bloodline** who would return to defeat evil again.
Shianndrea is that prophesied **"Chosen One"**.
The Emperor used to be one of us, a ninja of the Toshigawa Clan. Shianndrea is his daughter.
He too has **devastating** powers, and she is the only one who can bring an end to his reign.

If he harms her, he would be **unstoppable,** and the world would surely fall.
That is why we must move quickly if we are going to get Shianndrea out of there **before** the Emperor makes his move.
We should go in as a smaller unit.
The less lives we have to worry about, the better our chances of getting in and out
A small band against the entirety of the Azumi Ninja Camp?
That is suicide.
Who will this **strike team** be, Kim?
You're looking at it, **Mom.**
WE WILL BRING HER BACK.

PAGE 2

You finally awaken.
It is about time.
Soon you will be delivered into the hands of the Emperor and this world will fall.
I will have much to feed upon.
Even you depend on my capture.
Right now, the entire Azumi Ninja Clan is preparing to wipe your people off the face of the earth.
Believe me, there are many who will rejoice in your passing, girl.
PAGE 3

Just how powerful is Shianndrea supposed to be?
No one knows.
Only my father has been witness to her gift.
So this could all be some sort of superstitious theory?
Kinda like the Y2k bug?
I believe my father, Ai.
That is enough for me.

CRUNCH!!!!
ARGHA!

Woah woah WOAH!!
What do you think you're doing?
Here. Put these on.

You can't expect me to wear this. It's a guy's uniform.
By the time anyone would be in range to spot you, they would already be eliminated.
You too, Ai.
Great.

HEY!!!

PAGE 5

What's wrong with your uniforms?
You're clearly out of regulation, young lady.
Uh... Well.. we just..um so...
Wait. WHO ARE YOU?
KIM! CATCH HIM!!
Ok. That didn't work.
I thought you said no one would notice us.
No. I said that by the time they would be in range, they would be eliminated.
Now what?
These disguises won't get us past all of them.

It looks like the entire **Azumi clan** is out there.
They think we will be launching a full scale assault.
I assume that building by the watch tower is the entrance to the **prison area.**
PAGE 7

How are we going to get past all of them?
I'll distract them.
Kim, you make sure you get Shianndrea home **safely.**
No. We do this **together.**
You need someone to draw them **away.**
I can do that.
And we'll be **wiped out** together.
You're not going to take on an army by yourself, Ai.
I'll go with you.
Kim, you know what to do.
Do **not** take any chances out there.
If you see a chance to **escape**, you take it.
Sure, sure.
Since when does my **little brother** give the orders anyway?
Since I was born. Be careful.
Be careful.
I will.
Are you sure about this, Ai?
Yeah. I'll go out there.
Tell a few jokes.
We'll all **laugh.**
It's fine.
It's going to be... **good.**
PAGE 8

Ok, so what's the plan?
I have no idea.
You still have those explosive shurikens on you?
I think I have a few.
Bet you I can drop more of them than you can.
Ha! We'll see, Turra.
This should get their attention.
BOOM!!
THERE!! THE TOSHIGAWA ARE HERE!
OPEN FIRE!!
PAGE 9

WHOA! Those are some angry ninja!

That was just a **distraction,** Turra.

We've got company!

THIS IS WHERE THE FUN BEGINS!

SMACK!

SMASH!!

KIAH!

SMACK!

CRASH!!!

Shianndrea!

SMASH!!
Shianndrea! We've got to get you out of here.
No.
What do you mean, "no"?
We do not have much time.
Our people die.
Kokoro's clan is starving.
And I seem to be the cause of it all.
If I stay here... go with my father... maybe this will stop.
No more pain on my account.
No more... loneliness.
You cannot believe that.
Do you know how important you are?
Everyone keeps telling me.
But no, I'm not.
Ai and Turra are out there right now holding off an army for you, and Hamasuke almost died trying to save you.
We do not do this because you are some "chosen one".
You are our friend, first and foremost.
We all care about you, and we all need you.
I need you, Shianndrea.
Come on. We will get you out of here.
NGAH!
KIM!!

You are officially **more trouble** than you are worth, **little kunoichi.**
PAGE 13

Are...
Are we
done yet?
Doesn't
look like it.

I think they
were just a
warm up.
Really?
I thought we
would be able to
call it a day.

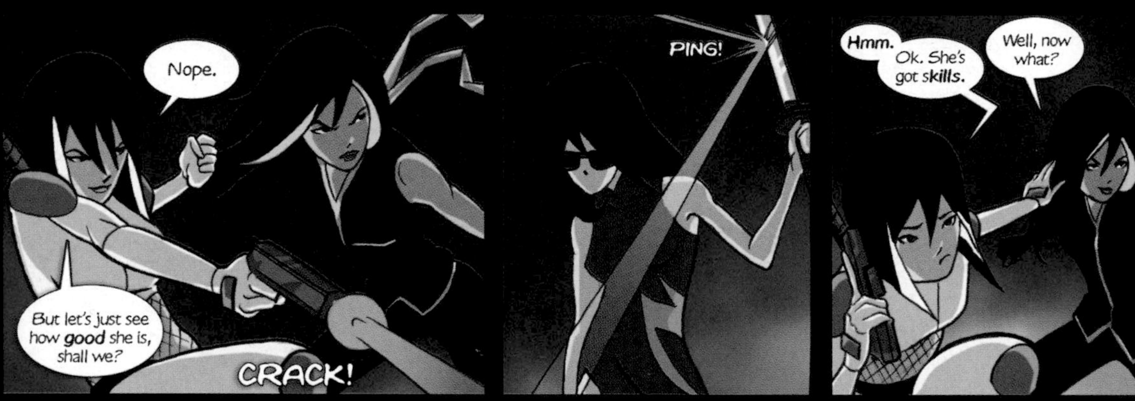
Nope.
But let's just see
how good she is,
shall we?
CRACK!
PING!
Hmm.
Ok. She's
got skills.
Well, now
what?

Well...now
we get to
play!

KEEP THE PRESSURE UP!
She's FAST!
UNGHA!
NO!
AI!!
Finally, we're alone.
Now we have a chance to talk, Turra.
Just you and I.
PAGE 15

YOU DON'T KNOW ME, LADY!!
YOU DON'T KNOW WHO YOU'RE DEALING WITH!!!
Wrong. I know exactly who you are, Turra.
I've watched you for some time now.
You are a very skilled fighter with a free spirit.
You are the best swords-woman in the Toshigawa.
You are also very easy to anger.
That anger causes you to make mistakes.
It reminds me of myself when I was younger.
What do you want?
Only for you to come see me again when you are ready to stop playing and start training.

You... You hurt him.
Perhaps the Emperor would accept you partially harmed.
I mean, your friend there came for you.
I subdued him.
I had to subdue you, too.
You...
Y'know, it would be sort of like a plot from some teen angst vampire movie.
Love. Loss. Tragedy.
It would fit perfectly.
And a ninja princess who just can't keep her boyfriends alive.
YOU HURT HIM!
PAGE 17

Hey...
HEY NOW!

ARGHA!!!

CRASH!

uggh...

WHOA!

Master?!

Master?!

Master?!

Master?!

Shianndrea?

Wait.
It is alright.
We...
Let us go
home.

NO!

NO!
STOP HER!
THE PRISONER!
ULP!
NO!
CRUNCH!
FWAP!
NO!
NGAH!
NO!

NO!

SLAM!!

She is mine!
This is as far as you go, girl.
GRRRR!
At least you will have company when I put you back into your cell.
COUGH!
OOOF!
Shianndrea. It's me. Kim.
You are going to be alright.
Kim?
She has passed out!
Grab Ai a
let's get o
of here.
The Azumi are regroup-ing!
PAGE 22

NOT AGAIN!
thunk
BOOM!!
And you thought you wouldn't **need** us on this mission, Kim.
CYAN? MEGUMI!!
I have never been so **happy** that someone **dis-obeyed** my orders.
I aim to **please.**
We've cut a path out of here.
Good! Let's vanish, ninja! Our work is **done** here.

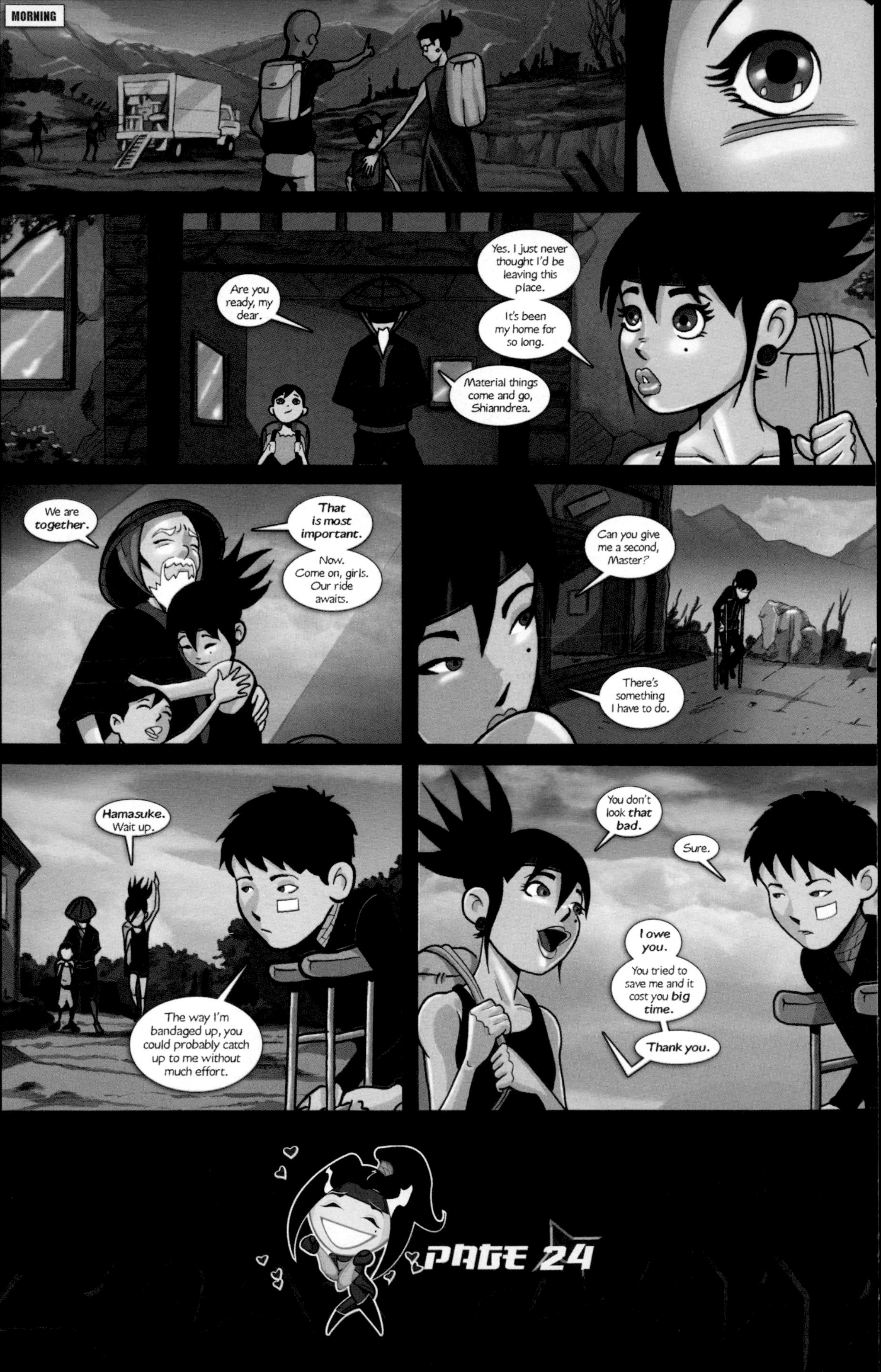

MORNING

Hamasuke. Wait up.

The way I'm bandaged up, you could probably catch up to me without much effort.

You don't look **that bad**.

Sure.

I owe you.

You tried to save me and it cost you **big time.**

Thank you.

Anything for the **ninja princess.**

She was **unstoppable.**

But she could not control it.

She does not even **remember** anything past me finding her in the cell.

Not her power.

Not the fight with the Oni.

None of it.

For now, that is **best.**

This will give us more time to train her to control her abilities

I'm afraid for her, Dad. She was a **force of nature.**

We couldn't even stop her.

What will that type of power do to someone so young?

How do we help her?

The Azumi ninja **witnessed** her transformation, Father.

If Kokoro **survived,** I'm sure he will be more **motivated** than ever to get his hands on Shianndrea.

We **train** her.

We **protect** her.

We **love** her.

Just as we **always** have.

I leave him for **five minutes** and the entire plan goes up in **flames.**
Kokoro's failure will be greatly **punished** by the Emperor if we do not **intervene.**
That girl must be **destroyed.**
We will not be **stopped,** old woman.

The original **contract** states to find Shianndrea Toshigawa.
That's not part of the plan.
If we kill her, we will bring the **ire** of the **Emperor.**
If you are **changing** your mind about why we are doing this, young one—
--No, Mother.
Good.

I will **conjure** a new, more powerful Oni to combat this girl's **dark powers.**
Very good.
And I will assume **leadership** of the Azumi Ninja.
Our revenge on the **Toshigawa lineage** will finally be realized and the world **will tremble.**
THE BEGINNIN

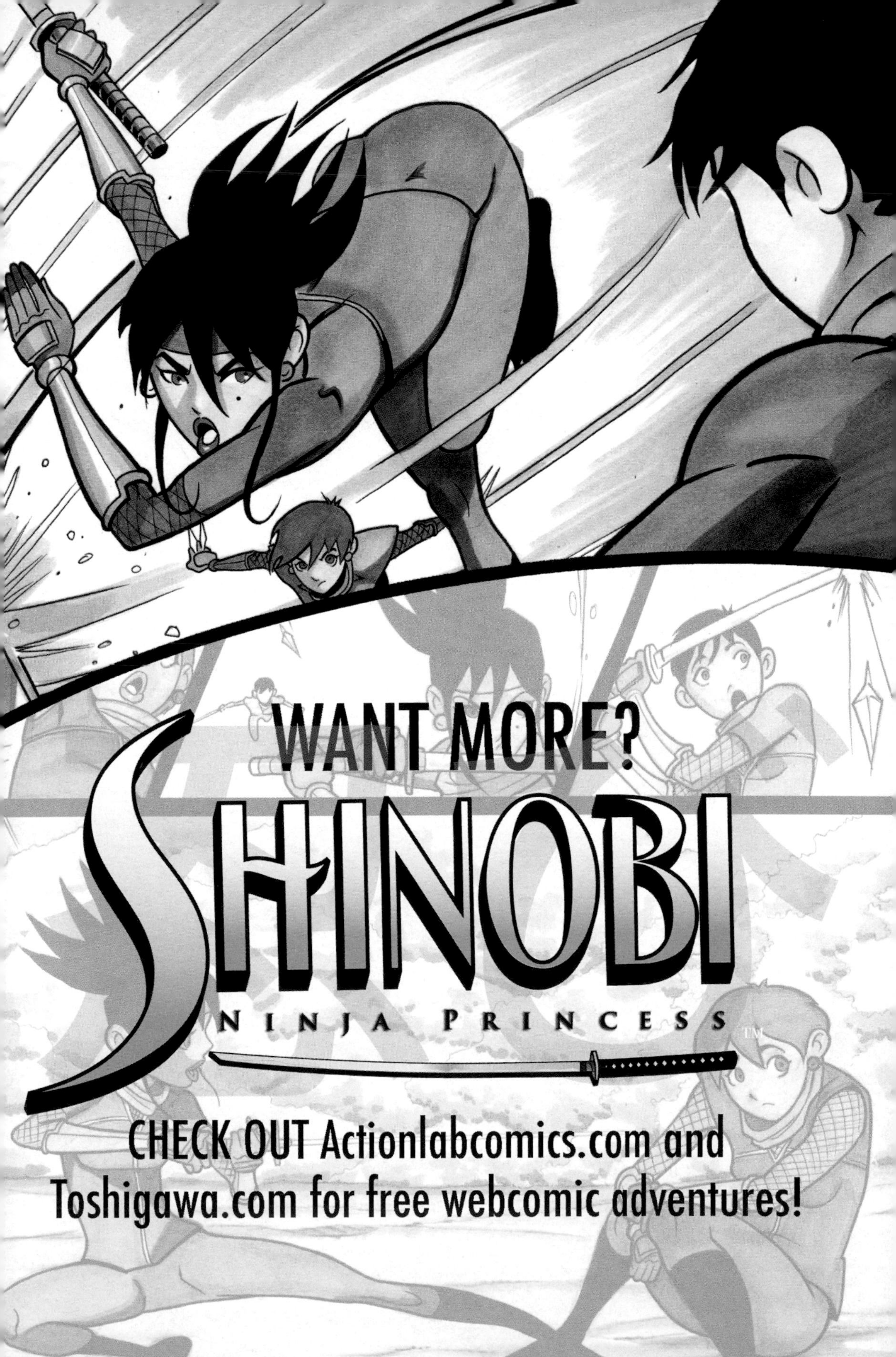
WANT MORE?
SHINOBI
NINJA PRINCESS ™
CHECK OUT Actionlabcomics.com and
Toshigawa.com for free webcomic adventures!

ELSEWHERE

MASTER, Your daughter has escaped capture again.
Kokoro and the Azumi Ninja have failed.
I know.
GOOD.
We will continue to allow them to give her the battle **experience** she needs in order to become **more powerful.**
Once her true power is **achieve** we will enact **phase two** of the plan.
WE WILL HAVE OUR REVENGE

NEXT: THE LIGHTING ONI

NEW FRIENDS. NEW ENEMIES. NEW ADVENTURE!
LAB
Princeless
ON SALE NOW!

Soft Spots™
available at
Toys"R"Us
36 puppies to collect with secret messages to share!
And look for the Soft Spots Magazine from Action Lab!
ACTION LAB
ACTIONLABCOMICS